THE
CAREER TRANSITION
POCKETBOOK

By Keith Corbin *Drawings by Phil Hailstone*

"This pocketbook provides a systematic and pragmatic approach to career transition.
A must for anyone, at any stage or turning point in their career."
Joan Porter-Butler, Employee Relations Manager (UK), Gap

"An excellent book, comprehensive and concise – ideal for readers looking for tips and guidance
as they progress their careers."
Colin Dalby, Head of Human Resources, Thomas Cook

"Over 30 years I have recruited a great number of people and conducted far too many interviews.
I wish all my applicants had read this book and followed Keith's advice."
Len Tunnicliffe, Account Director, Teradata, a Division of NCR

"At last, a concise and clear guide to career transition. A must have book
for anyone considering a new challenge."
Simon Leach, Market Development, Travelex PLC

Published by:
Management Pocketbooks Ltd
Laurel House, Station Approach, Alresford, Hants SO24 9JH, U.K.
Tel: +44 (0)1962 735573 Fax: +44 (0)1962 733637
E-mail: sales@pocketbook.co.uk
Website: www.pocketbook.co.uk

British Library Cataloguing-in-Publication Data – A catalogue record for this book is available
from the British Library.

ISBN 1 903776 01 5

Design, typesetting and graphics by **efex ltd** Printed in U.K.

CONTENTS

While we are postponing, life speeds by. Seneca (3BC - 65AD)

INTRODUCTION

THE IMPACT OF CHANGE

This Career Transition Pocketbook is for those of you who have found yourselves at a crossroads. You could have got there by yourself or you could have been placed there unwillingly to face the traffic on your own!

Changing your job or career is one of *the* major decisions you have to make in a lifetime. The change can be driven by you, or forced on you when you least expect it. The current reality for many of you is a world that is changing at a pace that, at times, can be very scary. For most, *what you do* is *who you are*. Your job or your career tends to shape how you live your life. Some current realities:

- Understand that NO job/career is for life!
- The global economy can sometimes have a major impact on your job security
- A deteriorating environment has knock-on effects on world markets and hence jobs
- International politics is not only volatile but sometimes it can seriously affect your job and standard of living
- For the foreseeable future there are always going to be *booms* and *busts*, eg: the e-business and telecoms boom and spectacular bust of 2000 - 2001

Be ready to react positively if one of the above realities begins to affect you.

INTRODUCTION

A WORD OF CAUTION!

There is a well-known truism that goes: *Looking for a new job/career is a full-time job in itself*. Making that career change can be daunting, time-consuming, frustrating and hard work. If you are not totally committed do not start! Landing up in a job that does not use all your skills or one that is taking you nowhere is usually a recipe for disaster and more frequent job searching.

Now let's look forward. Imagine what job/career success looks like:

- An interesting job with good career prospects
- Working with a group of people you enjoy being with
- You work really well with your boss
- You find that you are always learning new things
- One success leads to another success
- People look up to you and your reputation soars
- You are doing something that makes a difference

PURPOSE OF THIS POCKETBOOK

This book has been written to:
- Help you if you are at a crossroads (thinking about a job/career change)
- Guide you if you have had a job change enforced on you through redundancy/restructure or downsizing
- Assist you if you want to *brush-up* on your job search skills
- Provide a coaching road-map for managers and team-leaders who have to coach others on changing career direction
- Take the fear out of taking the *first step* when considering a career change
- Offer some practical tips and advice on how to use technology when job changing and job hunting; recruitment is now increasingly Internet dominated
- Be used by trainers, managers and human resource managers on workshops as a compact guide to career transition
- Act as a *last minute* source of helpful information prior to an important promotion interview or vital job interview

Before everything else, getting ready is the secret of success. — **Henry Ford**

SEVEN STEPS TO CAREER TRANSITION

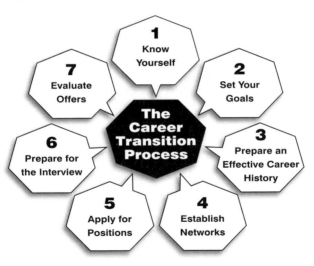

INTRODUCTION

CAREER TRANSITION IS A SIMPLE PROCESS!

The seven most important steps to making your career change are:

1. Know yourself
2. Set your goals
3. Prepare your most compelling career history
4. Establish your networks
5. Apply for positions
6. Prepare so well for the interview that you are better than anyone else
7. Evaluate your offers

If you haven't made the change you are looking for after the first run through the sequence, go through the steps again, evaluating your experience and deciding on new goals and methods. Then follow up these decisions with action.

Repeat this cycle until you make the change, eg: find a new job, gain promotion, change careers, become self-employed, start your own business, do voluntary work or retire.

Change alone is eternal, perpetual and immortal.   **Arthur Schopenhauer**

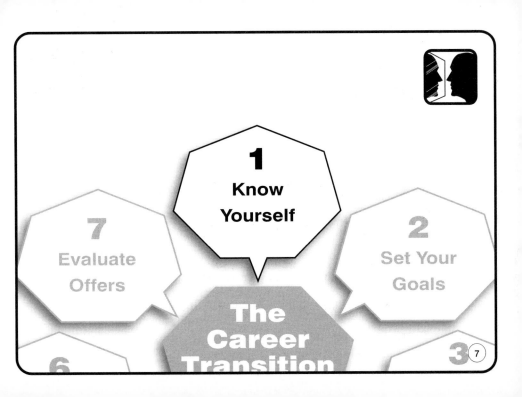

INITIAL QUESTIONS

Your career transition starts with you asking some vitally important questions about yourself:

- Who are you?
- Where are you now?
- Why do you want to change?
- What changes do you want?
- What skills do you need to make those changes?
- What do you want to do next?
- How do you put it all together?

When one door closes another door opens; but we so often look so long and so regretfully upon the closed door, that we do not see the ones which open for us.

Helen Keller

STEP 1 - KNOW YOURSELF

WHO ARE YOU?

Before you start your career transition it is really important to know yourself.
Be honest about your strengths and your weaknesses. As you progress you will soon begin to realise how important knowing yourself is to your future success.

On the journey to career success, recognising that you are a unique product means understanding:

- Your personality – the way you behave in the world
- Your attitude to others and to life in general
- Your skills and achievements
- Your values
- How you learn and take in information
- Your interests
- Your hopes and plans for the future

Before you talk about what you want - really appreciate what you have before it's gone. **Ethan Daniel**

STEP 1 - KNOW YOURSELF

WHO ARE YOU?

Start by considering some questions and writing down your thoughts:

- Who am I?
- What words would I use to describe myself?
- What am I like?
- How do others see me?
- How would others describe me?
- When I am being positive I am…? Make a list of *I am* statements.
- When I am being negative I am…? Make a list of *I am* statements.
- Using the prompt list on the next page write down as many words as you can to describe yourself.
- Ask close friends or relatives to confirm or challenge your descriptive words.

 Tip! Try these useful free websites: www.careerstorm.com/ or www.nextsteps.org or http://id60.reed.co.uk/id60.html

WHO ARE YOU?

COMPETITIVE
MODEST
STABLE

CLEAR-THINKING
METHODICAL
SINCERE
COMPETENT

CONSIDERATE
DEMONSTRATIVE
ACCURATE
RESOURCEFUL
EMPATHETIC

DISCREET
PERSUASIVE
UNCRITICAL
EVEN-TEMPERED

ABLE TO FOCUS,
ANIMATED, PUNCTUAL, ABLE
TO MANAGE PRESSURE/
STRESS

READY
FOR ACTION
RETICENT
STEADY

OUTGOING
THOROUGH
INQUIRING
TOLERANT
HELPFUL

REFLECTIVE
AMBITIOUS
IMAGINATIVE

WHO ARE YOU?

- When you think you have built up an accurate picture of yourself, choose the top 10 words that you believe describe you in the most positive way
- For each word give an example of when you used this strength in a positive way
- Think of what you said
- Think of what happened when you used that quality

Example

	Top 10 Attributes	Example of what it achieved
1	**Persuasive**	When I worked in marketing for xyz plc I got promoted because of the persuasive quality of my product reports. My manager would always ask me to help him develop his client presentations and most of the others in the team would ask my advice on what words and graphics to use in their reports.
2	**Organised**	

 Tip! Type in FREE PERSONALITY TESTS on any good internet search engine to find lots of sites offering free tests to help with your self-assessment.

WHAT SKILLS DO YOU NEED TO MAKE THOSE CHANGES?

A dictionary definition for the word SKILL (noun): *a special ability to do something*.

Think about all the skills that:
- You have now – they are your building blocks for the future
- You use at work, college, home, clubs, societies, etc
- You can easily apply in another job/career, ie: your transferable skills
- You used in all the things you are proud of or that gave you pleasure, ie: your achievements

Think too about:
- What you like doing
- What you are good at
- Something you did well, and what people said about you

> *There isn't a person anywhere that isn't capable of doing more than he thinks he can.*

Henry Ford

WHAT SKILLS DO YOU NEED TO MAKE THOSE CHANGES?

A BRIEF A-Z OF SKILLS

The list of skills (action words) below and on the following pages is invaluable for helping you to focus on what you do. These words will be very useful for putting together your Career History/Career Plan/CV/Resumé/Letters and for describing yourself at interviews. You will need to refer to them time and again.

A
achieving
acting
adapting
addressing
adjusting
administering
advising
altering
analysing
appraising
arbitrating
arranging
assembling

assessing
auditing

B
balancing
broadening
budgeting
building

C
calculating
calibrating
cataloguing
categorising

chairing
changing
charting
checking
classifying
co-ordinating
coaching
collating
collecting
combining
communicating
comparing
compiling
completing

composing
computing
conceiving
concluding
conducting
configuring
considering
consolidating
constructing
contracting
contrasting
creating

D
deciding
decreasing
defining
delegating
delivering
demonstrating
describing
designing
detecting
determining
developing
devising
diagnosing

WHAT SKILLS DO YOU NEED TO MAKE THOSE CHANGES?

A BRIEF A-Z OF SKILLS

D
dissecting
distributing
diverting
documenting
doubling
drafting
drawing

E
editing
eliminating
empathising
encouraging
enforcing
enhancing
enlarging
ensuring
establishing
estimating
evaluating

examining
expanding

F
fabricating
facilitating
filing
financing
finalising
fixing
following
forecasting
formulating
founding

G
gathering
giving
generating
guiding

H
hiring
hosting

I
identifying
illustrating
implementing
improving
improvising
incorporating
increasing
informing
initiating
inspecting
installing
instituting
instructing
integrating
interacting
interpreting
interviewing

J
judging

L
launching
learning
lecturing
liaising
listing
locating

M
maintaining
managing
marking
marketing
measuring
mediating
meeting
minimising
modelling
moderating

modernising
modifying
monitoring
motivating

N
narrating
navigating
negotiating

O
observing
obtaining
opening
operating
ordering
organising
orienting
originating

WHAT SKILLS DO YOU NEED TO MAKE THOSE CHANGES?

A BRIEF A-Z OF SKILLS

P
painting
performing
persuading
photographing
piloting
planning
predicting
preparing
prescribing
presenting
printing
processing
producing
programming
projecting
promoting
proof-reading
proposing
protecting
providing

publicising
publishing
purchasing

Q
quantifying
qualifying

R
raising
receiving
recommending
reconciling
recording
recruiting
redesigning
reducing
referring
refining
rehabilitating
relating
rendering

reorganising
repairing
reporting
restructuring
retrieving
reviewing
revising
revitalising

S
scheduling
searching
securing
selecting
separating
serving
servicing
setting
sewing
shaping
sharing

showing
simplifying
sizing
sketching
selling

T
talking
teaching
tending
testing
tracing
training
transcribing
transforming
translating
travelling
treating
trimming
trouble-shooting
tutoring

U
uncovering
unifying
updating
upgrading
using
utilising

V
verifying

W
weighing
welding
widening
winning
writing

TEAMWORKING SKILLS/ACTIVITIES

If you manage a team of people or work as part of a team, here are some of the skills you might use on a frequent basis:

Appraising people   Coaching   Controlling   Counselling

Budgeting   Communicating   Co-ordinating

Decision-making   Delegating   Developing self and others   Estimating

Forecasting

Generating ideas   Influencing   Innovating   Leading

Listening   Managing projects   Interviewing   Leading meetings

Mentoring   Motivating   Negotiating

Organising   Planning

Resolving conflict   Presenting   Problem-solving   Report writing

Training   Risk-taking   Setting objectives   Teambuilding

WHAT ARE YOUR TOP SKILLS & ABILITIES?

An example of a skills list:

1. Leadership skills (major skill area, especially motivating and coaching)	6. Managing budgets
	7. Negotiating
2. Flexibility (adapting to most situations and people)	8. Developing other people
	9. Writing reports
3. Generating new ideas (creative skills)	10. Making presentations to groups of people
4. Performing well under stress	
5. Selling	

Categorise your transferable skills.

Tip! List as many examples as you can of how you have used each of these skills - at work, school, home, during leisure activities, voluntary work, etc.

> *To find out what one is fitted to do and to secure an opportunity to do it is the key to happiness.*
>
> **John Dewey**

YOUR ACHIEVEMENTS

Having identified your key skills, the next most important items on your career transition plan are the achievements which you enjoyed and from which you gained success.

Review your career to date and summarise your personal achievements. These achievements demonstrate your key skills that will be important to consider when developing your career plan.

The list of achievements will also provide a useful reminder of those things that you will probably want to highlight during job interviews.

No bird soars too high if he soars with his own wings.

William Blake

19

YOUR ACHIEVEMENTS

QUANTIFY THEM

Whenever possible **quantify** your achievements. For example:

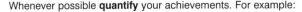

- Increased regional sales volumes during a financial year by over 17% despite a very flat market

- Improved customer retention and arrears collections by over 20% in a 6-month period – saving the company at least £5,000

- Introduced Standard Operating Procedures to the North West region

- Launched new sales and payments propositions to the sales force

- Launched new profit and loss accounts processes throughout the region

- Project-managed the most comprehensive organisation development programme (The People Like Us - PLUS - Programme) undertaken by xyz plc in its history

- Over a 6-month period project-managed the implementation of a radical new PC-based Management Information reporting system which decreased month end reporting time from 10 days to 1 day – resulting in an annual cost saving of £50,000

STEP 1 - KNOW YOURSELF

WHAT DO YOU VALUE IN LIFE & WORK?

Thinking about what you want from work and life is an important part of successful career transition. Which of the following value words and statements do you:

A. Like very much?   **B.** Like?   **C.** Dislike a lot?

Giving back to society	Working by yourself	Adventure	Moral fulfilment
Change and variety	Acknowledgement	Influencing people	Inventive work
Helping others	Competing with others	Financial gain	Community
Precision work	Fast pace	Learning new things	Managing people and resources
Contact with people	Making your own decisions	Physical challenge	Work and life balance
Stability	Stimulation	Becoming an expert	
Working with a team	Working under pressure	Independence	
Job security		Artistic creativity	

Think seriously about the above values. Place them in priority order, and make a list of your top five values.

The greatest use of life is to spend it for something that outlasts it. **William James**

21

AND NOW THE FINAL PICTURE!

You have carried out your self-assessment. It is now time to summarise what you have to offer another employer or promotion board. Alternatively, you may choose to use the information you have gathered about yourself to consider whether or not to set up your own business.

Think of what you have to offer as a brain map.

- Personality and attitudes
- Skills and achievements
- Values
- Interests
- Your most important strengths

 Tip! To help you focus on the entire topic of this chapter, try this really brilliant website: http://www.cdm.uwaterloo.ca/

FIRST RECOGNISE A CHANGING ENVIRONMENT

- The conditions you will face in your career transition are vastly different from those experienced by former generations

- It is important to recognise that there are major changes taking place in the work environment

- The changes will also affect those you are seeking to influence, eg: potential employers

- These changes are the result of social, economic and technological factors that impact on all organisations

- Understanding this changing environment can improve your ability to make your career transition a successful one

CAREER TRANSITION GOAL SETTING

Career transition goal setting demands that you first make an informed career choice, ie: *What do I want?*

- Career transition requires you to make use of accurate and up-to-date occupational information

- Career decision-making is directly related to your knowledge of yourself – your values, interests, temperament, financial needs, physical work requirements or limitations

- The effects of past experiences, new information, and changes in your current life situation and environment all interconnect

- You should continually review decisions you've already made and consider decisions yet to be made

- Good decision-making requires you to engage in a formal process, ie: committed to paper or hard-disk

YOUR CAREER DECISION-MAKING PROCESS

1. Define your challenge
2. State it clearly
3. List the initial alternative solutions
4. Collect information and expand the list of alternatives
5. Compare several alternatives
6. Choose one alternative
7. Take action on your choice
8. Review
9. Make a new decision

YOUR CAREER DECISION-MAKING PROCESS

1. Define your challenge

Think of this as your *dream* challenge.

I want to:

- Get promoted
- Change jobs
- Find a job
- Work from home
- Work part-time

- Find a job in Europe
- Work in the *Not for Profit* sector
- Start a business
- Retire

YOUR CAREER DECISION-MAKING PROCESS

2. State your goal clearly

What outcome do you want from the challenge?

- I want to be promoted to a higher grade in the next six months, with at least a £1,500 increase in salary
- I am unhappy in this job; I want to change jobs by July of this/next year
- I want to return to work now that Matthew is eighteen months old
- I want to give something back to society so I am going to start looking for work in the *Not for Profit* sector in the South East
- I want to apply to 25 large companies (more than 200 employees) within 30 miles of Rugby that might be looking for trainee accountants

YOUR CAREER DECISION-MAKING PROCESS

3. List your initial alternative solutions

Think about your contingencies should your goal not work out.

If I am not successful at gaining promotion I can:

- Try again for the same in six months
- Leave the company
- Try for a different type of job in three months
- Find a coach/mentor to help me succeed
- Complain to the union/my boss
- Do nothing

STEP 2 - SET YOUR GOALS

YOUR CAREER DECISION-MAKING PROCESS

4. Collect information and develop the list of choices

I am unhappy in this job; I want to change jobs by July of this/next year.

1. What kind of information do you need?
- What have I got to offer?
- What jobs are out there now?
- Where are they?
- What are these employers looking for?

2. Where can you obtain it?
- Networking
- Newspapers and other media
- Internet job sites
- Recruitment agencies

3. Is it relevant to the problem?
- Yes, it is relevant to what I want to happen
- I can start doing something

YOUR CAREER DECISION-MAKING PROCESS

5. Compare and think seriously about your choices

- What you know about yourself, ie: your values
  - Have I done all the self-assessment?
  - Do I know my skills, values, achievements, etc?
  - Can I do this job?
- Your commitments to others involved in the change
  - Who else will it affect (eg: partner, children, parents, friends)?
  - What impact will it have on them (eg: if we move then the children will have to change schools)?
- Your resources
  - Can I/we afford the change, ie: the cost of houses in the new area?
  - Can I cope with commuting three hours every day?
- Your constraints
  - Is the timing right?
  - Will it mean a move?
  - Will the children want to move?
  - Will Sam find a job when we move?

YOUR CAREER DECISION-MAKING PROCESS

6. Choose one alternative

- I am going to apply for the job I saw in the newspaper today

7. Take action on your choice

- Analyse the job
- Update your CV
- Draft the letter of application
- Research the job
- Prepare for the interview

8. Review

- Review your actions frequently

9. Make new decisions if necessary

- If you are not going to be offered an interview then start again

YOUR JOB/CAREER INTERESTS

- Over the years, as you mature and gain experience, you will develop preferences for certain types of work and working environments

- People who enjoy their jobs usually have an interest in what they do

- If, for example, you have a genuine interest in working with people, then you will be motivated to find a job that involves you with people

- If you really like working with figures then you are likely to look for a job that requires number skills

YOUR JOB/CAREER INTERESTS

The psychologist John Holland developed a very useful group of occupational categories. He found that people's interests drew them to particular types of occupation. Moreover, people in the same occupation (but not necessarily with the same values) tended to have similar skills and interests.

His interest types were called:

- Realistic
- Investigative
- Artistic
- Social
- Enterprising
- Conventional

Tip!
1) A great website based on Holland's work is http://www.careerkey.org/english. It will help you think through your interests/career options and it's free!
2) Also try www.gov.nf.ca/nlwin - another good site for career options.

Further useful information about vocational choices is available at http://www.derby.ac.uk/careers/workout/index.htm. Register then work your way through this challenging analysis!

HOLLAND'S INTEREST TYPES

Realistic
- Likes to work with animals, tools or machines; generally avoids social activities like teaching, counselling, nursing, and informing others
- Has good skills in working with tools, mechanical drawings, machines or animals
- Values practical things you can see and touch, likes plants and animals; sees self as practical, mechanical and realistic

Investigative
- Likes to study/solve mathematical or scientific problems; generally avoids leading, selling or persuading people
- Has good skills at understanding and solving scientific or mathematical problems
- Values science; sees self as precise, scientific and intellectual

Artistic
- Likes to do creative activities like art, drama, crafts, dance, music and creative writing; generally avoids highly ordered or repetitive activities
- Has good artistic abilities – in creative writing, drama, crafts, music or art
- Values the creative arts – like drama, music, art or literature; sees self as expressive

HOLLAND'S INTEREST TYPES

Social
- Likes to do things to help people – like teaching, counselling, nursing or giving information; generally avoids using machines, tools or animals to achieve a goal
- Has good skills at teaching, counselling, nursing or giving information
- Values helping people and solving social problems; sees self as helpful, friendly and trustworthy

Enterprising
- Likes to lead and persuade people, and to sell things and ideas; generally avoids activities that require careful observation and scientific, analytical thinking
- Is good at leading people and selling things or ideas
- Values success in politics, leadership or business; sees self as energetic, ambitious and sociable

Conventional
- Likes to work with numbers, records or machines in a set, orderly way; generally avoids ambiguous, unstructured activities
- Is good at working with written records and numbers in a systematic, orderly way
- Values success in business; sees self as orderly and good at following a set plan

STEP 2 - SET YOUR GOALS

LOOK BEFORE YOU LEAP!

A good model to help you think about change!

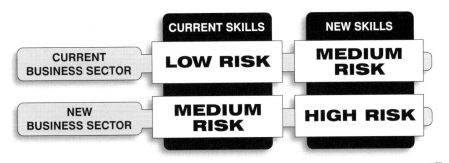

	CURRENT SKILLS	NEW SKILLS
CURRENT BUSINESS SECTOR	LOW RISK	MEDIUM RISK
NEW BUSINESS SECTOR	MEDIUM RISK	HIGH RISK

STEP 2 - SET YOUR GOALS

OPTIONS FOR CHANGE

LOW RISK

Low Risk Option

- The low risk option is seeking a job similar to your current/last position, in the same industry sector (eg: a travel consultant moves from one travel chain to another)

- You may already have useful contacts in your work area: use them to network and identify new opportunities

OPTIONS FOR CHANGE

MEDIUM RISK   Medium Risk Option

1. New skills, same business sector
- For example, moving from a quality assurance role in the food sector to technical training with another food company
- This may involve retraining: are you prepared for this?
- Would your personal circumstances allow you to study?
- Can you afford the costs of retraining?
- Are you still physically and intellectually capable of the change?
- Are you at a relatively early stage in your career and how well do you know your own sector?
- Have you identified a potential skill shortage?
- The long-term benefits may well be worth the initial financial sacrifice

2. Same skills, new business sector
- Eg: an accountant can move relatively easily from the food sector to the travel industry
- Some skills, experience and competencies can also lead you into consultancy work of various kinds

STEP 2 - SET YOUR GOALS

OPTIONS FOR CHANGE

HIGH RISK   **High Risk Option**

- The high risk option is choosing to develop new skills and market them in a new business sector
- For most people this is both impractical and unrealistic (a quality manager becoming a brain surgeon!)
- For others it may be achievable by taking it a stage at a time
- For example, moving into the same role within a new business sector might then lead to you switching roles once you have established yourself in that new area
- If you really have an all-consuming desire to retrain as a school teacher or as a psychotherapist then following the advice in this book should help you to make that big step
- Changing direction completely is not always impossible and in many cases may be the result of you taking a long hard look at yourself and re-appraising what you really want to do with the rest of your life

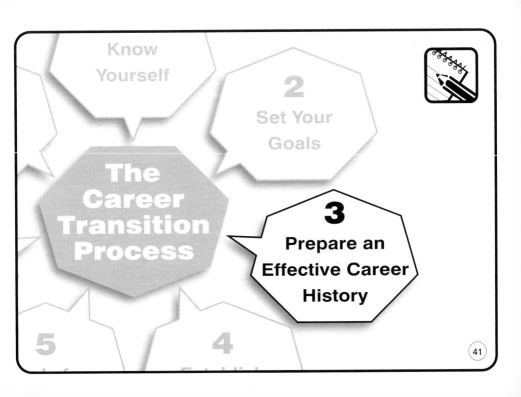

STEP 3 - PREPARE AN EFFECTIVE CAREER HISTORY

WHAT YOU HAVE LEARNT SO FAR

Well done on carrying out that important work of self-discovery!

You have now completed steps one and two. You now
know more about:

- Yourself and how others see you
- Your skills
- Your achievements
- Your values
- Setting some goals
- Making some choices

You can now begin to make plans to
put all this new knowledge to good use.

STEP 3 - PREPARE AN EFFECTIVE CAREER HISTORY

WHAT IS A CAREER HISTORY?

Your career history is your:

- Marketing tool
- Unique Selling Point (USP)
- Personal advertisement to the world of work
- Personal web page

Also known as:

- Your Curriculum Vitae (CV)
- In North America – your resumé

WHAT IS YOUR CAREER HISTORY?

Think of your career history as one of the most important pieces of information you have to produce.

It's as crucial as your:

- Birth certificate
- Driving licence
- Passport

Your career history is your passport to success!

Having an accurate representation of yourself helps you gain entry to the job or career you want!

STEP 3 - PREPARE AN EFFECTIVE CAREER HISTORY

AIM TO GRAB ATTENTION!

Your aim is to ensure that your career history is so compelling that it shouts at the reader: **READ ME!**

Imagine, when busy managers or human resource managers are recruiting they may have fifty or more CVs to read. This means you probably have about 30 - 45 seconds in which to catch their attention! Make absolutely sure that your CV is firmly placed on the **yes** pile.

WHAT DOES *READ ME!* MEAN?

It means ensuring that your CV is:

- Visual
- Eye-catching and easy to read
- Easy to follow with sufficient white space
- Not too long nor too short – certainly no more than two pages
- Interesting, attractive, informative, professional, factual
- So interesting, in fact, that it obliges the reader to say to himself/herself – *I must meet this person!*

BASIC LAYOUT OF YOUR CAREER HISTORY

Name and Address
Telephone/fax/mobile/
e-mail address

(Profile)

(A list of skills and
achievements)

(Career summary)

(Education and training)

(Professional memberships)

(Personal information)

- Short paragraph describing what you have to offer the employer

- Detailed account of those skills, activities and achievements that best represent your suitability for the job in question (must be results oriented)

- Complete history of your job experience including achievements (**not** job descriptions)

- Highest educational achievement first and anything else that is relevant to the role

- (if relevant)

- Include date of birth/age, marital status, nationality, driving licence details and interests (interests are optional; only include those that present another positive side to you; be wary of anything that might be seen as controversial)

STEP 3 - PREPARE AN EFFECTIVE CAREER HISTORY

A CHECKLIST

It must:

✓ Look professional and have immediate impact

✓ Contain crisp, concise and relevant personal information

✓ Immediately sell your skills and achievements, ie: the reader sees Results! Results! Results!

✓ Answer the reader's most problematical questions: 'Can you do the job?' 'Will you fit in?' 'Will I like you?'

✓ Appear complete at first reading, ie: a full history with no gaps

✓ Describe your relevant training and qualifications

✓ Look and feel right! – no spelling mistakes, typos or poor grammar

STEP 3 - PREPARE AN EFFECTIVE CAREER HISTORY

WHAT SHOULD *NOT* BE IN YOUR CAREER HISTORY

Title
No need to give your CV a title other than your name.

Salary
Do not include any reference to salary as this could exclude you from being considered for an interview by being too high or too low.

Reason for leaving
This can be difficult so save it for the interview – and only if asked directly. This gives you the chance of presenting the facts in the most positive light.

Photographs
Avoid unless specifically requested.

Personal
Exclude details about your physical appearance (height, weight, etc) and about religious/political affiliations that could be prejudicial.

WHAT SHOULD _NOT_ BE IN YOUR CAREER HISTORY

Referees

Make a note of the names, addresses and telephone numbers of your referees on a separate sheet and include only when you are asked to do so. You may wish to use different referees depending on the job you are applying for. Make sure you ask your referees if they are willing to act for you and keep them up to date on what is happening.

Gimmicks

Coloured paper or coloured ink may look good to you but will not bear the test of being photocopied, faxed or scanned. Binders will be ripped off and certainly do not encourage recruiters to 'keep you on file' as they will take up too much space. Too many frames or shaded boxes and odd typefaces may just obscure your message.

Humour

Definitely to be avoided in CVs and covering letters as it can so easily backfire. Keep your sense of humour for the interview when you can gauge your audience.

Tip! Leave out anything that might be used to exclude you from an interview shortlist

EXAMPLES OF CAREER HISTORIES

There are two main types – a **chronological CV** and a **functional CV**.

Chronological CV

This is the most accepted, uncomplicated and easy to prepare CV format. It provides the reader with a job/career history, educational and other important information in a logical, sequential order.

Some advantages	Some disadvantages
• Where your last employer is an important consideration, ie: a well-known company with a great reputation	• Where your work history has a number of gaps
• Where your next career move is in the same field as your previous jobs	• When you are looking for a career change or a move to a new business sector
• Where your career history shows a sustained upward path and career development	• Where your job changes might be seen as too frequent
• Where your former/existing job titles are in demand in the current job market	• Where you wish to avoid emphasising your age or where you have been doing the same job for a long time

EXAMPLES OF CAREER HISTORIES

Functional or skills-based CV

This format requires careful thought because you must group your skills into categories according to skill/competence/functional areas. It is a useful way of demonstrating your suitability for a job. See example of a functional CV on page 70.

Some advantages	Some disadvantages
• Where you wish to highlight specific skills/abilities and achievements to match the job you are applying for	• Tends to take a lot longer to think about and put together
• Where you are changing career direction or where much of your work has been freelance or consulting	• Where you have performed a limited number of functions in your jobs, ie: you don't have a wide range of transferable skills to offer
• Where you have held several jobs and would prefer to describe all your transferable skills	
• Where you are a graduate and want to include skills and responsibilities used during university, voluntary or unpaid work	• Your career path/job history is not shown until the second page
• Where your job record has been irregular through unemployment, redundancy, ill health, parenting, etc	• The style may not be to everyone's taste

STEP 3 - PREPARE AN EFFECTIVE CAREER HISTORY

STYLE MATTERS!

Your aim is to make the reader read on, so:

- Make your career history visually appealing
- Signpost with bold headings so that the reader knows where you are going
- Include sufficient white space but not too much
- Use an easy to read and common type font, eg:

> - Arial – abcdefghijklmnopqrstuvwxyz1234567890
> - Arial Narrow – abcdefghijklmnopqrstuvwxyz1234567890
> - Tahoma – abcdefghijklmnopqrstuvwxyz1234567890
> - Times New Roman – abcdefghijklmnopqrstuvwxyz1234567890

- Laser print the finished document for better quality

EXAMPLE TYPE FONTS

The font you
choose is a
matter of personal
preference but try
to keep it simple!

Arial example

Arial Narrow example

Times New Roman
example

Tahoma example

Simon Quinn
4 Abbey Drive, Quantock, Cambridgeshire, PE14 3QW
Daytime Tel: 020 8123 4567 Evening Tel: 01770 123456
e-mail: quinn2000@hotwire.com

Simon Quinn
4 Abbey Drive, Quantock, Cambridgeshire, PE14 3QW
Daytime Tel: 020 8123 4567 Evening Tel: 01770 123456
e-mail: quinn2000@hotwire.com

Simon Quinn
4 Abbey Drive, Quantock, Cambridgeshire, PE14 3QW
Daytime Tel: 020 8123 4567 Evening Tel: 01770 123456
e-mail: quinn2000@hotwire.com

Simon Quinn
4 Abbey Drive, Quantock, Cambridgeshire, PE14 3QW
Daytime Tel: 020 8123 4567 Evening Tel: 01770 123456
e-mail: quinn2000@hotwire.com

A STYLE TEMPLATE

1. Simon Quinn
   4 Abbey Drive, Quantock, Cambridgeshire, PE14 3QW
   Daytime Tel: 020 8123 4567 Evening Tel: 01770 123456
   e-mail: quinn2000@hotwire.com

2. An achievement-orientated trouble-shooter with Director level experience of driving major international change and profit improvement initiatives in the retail, travel and leisure industries.

3. Key skills

4. Career history

5. Main achievements

6. A chronological list of jobs – latest job first

7. Education, training and development

8. Personal details and interests

1. VISUAL SIGNPOSTING

Provide the reader with
quality contact information

Simon Quinn

4 Abbey Drive, Quantock, Cambridgeshire, PE14 3QW
Daytime Tel/fax: 020 8123 4567
Evening Tel: 01770 123456 mobile: 07999 123456
e-mail: quinn2000@hotwire.com

Ian Pringle BA (Hons.) C.Eng

77 Tintern Close,
Irton Wiston,
Peterborough
PE2 0XY
Tel: +44 (0)1733 888888
Fax: +44 (0)1733 888889
E-mail: ip@netcomuk.co.uk

If you have it – degrees, masters,
professional qualifications – flaunt it!

2. YOUR HEADLINE OR USP

Your headline or USP should provide an instant picture of what you have to offer! Try not to be too fancy, but do not undersell yourself! Some examples:

An achievement-orientated trouble-shooter with Director Level experience of driving major international change and profit improvement initiatives in the retail, travel and leisure industries.

An experienced and enthusiastic DESIGNER with an in-depth knowledge of all aspects of the product development process in production BOAT BUILDING gained over 12 years. Took a leading role in helping to establish the company as a leader in the UK market. Can demonstrate a highly successful track-record of directing a creative team of boat designers and technicians.

A professionally qualified and experienced PROJECT MANAGEMENT, PROCESS IMPROVEMENT, QUALITY and OPERATIONS specialist. Able to show a proven record of achievement in implementing change successfully, founded on broad-based technical experience, gained in a wide range of industrial, retail and commercial sectors.

STEP 3 - PREPARE AN EFFECTIVE CAREER HISTORY

3. SIGNPOST YOUR KEY SKILLS & EXPERIENCE

Examples of skills lists:

- Leading and developing multi-site and multi-channel retail distribution
- Conceiving and directing major strategic and operational change-management programmes at management level
- Analysing customer trends/financial data to improve margins and reduce costs
- Applying exceptional problem-solving and decision-making abilities

---

- Communicating strategy and influencing and inspiring teams at all levels
- Building and leading strong cross-functional and multi-cultural teams
- Effective people management and leadership skills
- Fluent oral and written communication skills

- Numerate and computer literate – MS Office, FrontPage, Quark Express
- Capable of planning, organising and implementing a wide range of complex projects
- An enthusiastic, energetic, self-motivated and thorough individual

 Tip! Very light shading of the main headings of your CV creates visual impact - but don't overdo it! Definitely no shading if you are intending to send your CV electronically

STEP 3 - PREPARE AN EFFECTIVE CAREER HISTORY

4. JOB HISTORY

- Signpost again – make it easy for the reader to see where you came from
- Start with the latest job first
- Always include a job title
- Be wary of leaving a big gap – explain the reason for the gap

A career history with different jobs in different companies:

05/00 TO PRESENT	THE CLOTHESLINE PLC	UK OPERATIONS PROJECT MANAGER
09/98 TO 04/00	B.H. BLACKS LTD	QUALITY & PROCESS MANAGER
09/94 TO 08/98	B.H. BLACKS LTD	COMPANY SERVICES OPERATIONS MANAGER
01/92 TO 09/94	B.H. BLACKS LTD	ORGANISATION & METHODS ANALYST
03/91 TO 12/91	WOOLCO PLC	ANALYST 'MERCHANDISE HANDLING' TEAM
09/89 TO 03/91	INGOT ALLOYS LTD	INDUSTRIAL ENGINEER
09/86 TO 09/89	INGOT ALLOYS LTD	COMMERCIAL APPRENTICE
07/85 TO 08/86	PGG CHARTERED ACCOUNTANTS	CLERK TO OFFICE MANAGER

4. JOB HISTORY

A career history with different jobs in the same company:

01 Jul 1979 **- 29 Sep 1995**	**TRAVEL GROUP LTD**
1994 - 1995	HR Consultant, New Directions Centre
1993 - 1994	Personnel Manager & Re-deployment Projects Manager
1990 - 1993	Personnel Manager, Retail Shops
1988 - 1990	Group Management Development Manager
1986 - 1988	Personnel Manager, Head Office, Peterborough
1979 - 1986	Regional Personnel Officer
1963 – 1978	Royal Navy
1962 – 1963	United Baltic Corporation

5. MAIN ACHIEVEMENTS

- The reader is looking for (and must see) – **RESULTS! RESULTS! RESULTS!**
- Wherever possible – **QUANTIFY, QUANTIFY, QUANTIFY**
- The reader is trying to find out – can you hit the ground running?

Example:

- Project-managed the external fact-finding audit by KPMG of XYZ plc's compliance to the 1998 Data Protection Act.
- Implemented a Global Store Opening Process (GSOP) in partnership with colleagues from New York HQ. The binder process was rolled out to 150 UK stores in February 2001.
- Applied a range of policy and procedure cost improvement measures, eg: in-store cash disbursement levels reduced from 0.18% of store turnover to 0.10% - equivalent to a saving of £320,000 p.a.
- Implemented management controls in merchandise handling, reducing damaged and defective stock by approximately 12.5% to £1.4 million p.a.

A long list of action words is given on pages 14-16 to help you quantify your achievements. Also, try this website: http://www.ucc.ie/careers/AdviceInfo/ApplicationsCVs/jobAppsCVs.html#key.

61

6. PAINT A PEN PICTURE OF YOUR JOBS

- Describe your most recent job first, then the job before that, then the one before that, etc
- Provide more information about your most recent jobs
- For jobs in the distant past, give a brief (single line) description only (the reader is usually more interested in what you can do now not 10 years ago)

Example of job with list of job-holder's achievements:

Regional Sales Manager: May 1998 – January 2001

Promoted to manage and develop teams of up to seven District Sales Managers, responsible for maximising the profitability of 85 retail shops, incorporating customer base of 300,000 with an annual turnover in excess of £40m.

- Increased regional sales volumes by over 17% in a flat market (1998/9)
- Improved customer retention and arrears collections by over 20% (1998/9)
- Introduced Standard Operating Procedures throughout the region
- Launched new sales and payments propositions to the sales force
- Launched profit and loss accounts processes throughout the region

6. PAINT A PEN PICTURE OF YOUR JOBS

Example of job with list of job-holder's achievements:

Director, U.K. Development: April 1998 – March 2001
Promoted to direct significant profit improvement initiatives and strategic change management programmes.

- Exceeded £32m profit improvement goal and all customer satisfaction targets.
- Led senior cross-functional teams with responsibility for all U.K. Sales, Productivity, Profit, Customer Service and CRM improvement programmes.
- Drove the U.K. multi-channel distribution strategy for Flights and component travel, leading to creation of travelgroup.com.
- Led joint venture negotiations with Independent Travel Agents that represents over 900 agencies throughout the U.K. This long-term relationship generated significant additional sales of £10m and support for Travel Group Holidays.
- Directed the design, development, trial and roll out of highly successful Travel Group Hypermarket stores (10,000 sq.ft. out of town travel hypermarkets), generating new sales of £35m.

63

7. EDUCATION, TRAINING & DEVELOPMENT

- Give the reader details of your education/qualifications
- Some companies take great care to check your qualifications – be warned!
- Include relevant training courses where they enhance the quality of your career history

EDUCATION & QUALIFICATIONS
- Post Graduate Diploma in Human Resource Strategies at the London Guildhall
- Graduate of the Chartered Institute of Personnel Development
- Institute of Direct Marketing Certificate in Call Centre Management - November 1997
- Colchester College of Art, Sept 1986 - June 1988, BTEC National Diploma, Clothing and Distributive Trades
- The Royal Masonic School for Girls, Rickmansworth, Hertfordshire, Sept 1979 - June 1986, 5 O levels

EDUCATION & QUALIFICATIONS

BA (Hons) Industrial Design (Transportation)	Coventry Polytechnic	1980-1984
4 GCE A levels	Hutton Grammar School	1978-1980
8 GCE O levels	Fulwood County High School	1973-1978

OTHER QUALIFICATIONS
ICC Motor Boat Helmsman, AutoCAD, Novell, Microsoft Office

8. PERSONAL DETAILS & INTERESTS

- This is the final important piece of information about you
- It tells the reader that you have another life outside work
- Best place to include your age if you think age will work against you
- Make it short and simple
- Warning – don't include anything that will put the reader off! (eg: membership of strange societies, political affiliations, religion, etc)

Tip! Try this website: http://www.calibrecandidates.com/cv_templates_more_experienced.html It provides you with a CV template to kick start the process.

PERSONAL DETAILS
Date of Birth: 01 June 1967
Status: Married with one daughter
Interests: Current Affairs, Travel, Sailing, Skiing, Tennis

PERSONAL DETAILS
Date of Birth: 02 August 1965
Status: Married with two daughters

INTERESTS AND ACTIVITIES
Travelling, reading, golf, jazz dance and cooking, voluntary school governor and mentor

EXAMPLE OF A CHRONOLOGICAL CV

Simon Quinn
4 Abbey Drive, Quantock, Cambridgeshire, PE14 3QW
Daytime Tel: 020 8123 4567 Evening Tel: 01770 123456 e-mail: quinn2000@hotwire.com

An achievement-orientated trouble-shooter with Director level experience of driving major international change and profit improvement initiatives in the retail, travel and leisure industries.

KEY SKILLS
- **Leading** and developing multi-site, multi-channel retail distribution businesses
- **Conceiving** and directing major strategic, operational change-management programmes at board level
- **Analysing** customer trends and financial data to improve margins, reduce costs and maximise profits
- **Applying** exceptional problem-solving and decision-making abilities
- **Communicating** strategy and influencing and inspiring teams at all levels
- **Building and leading** strong cross-functional, multi-cultural teams

CAREER HISTORY
THE TRAVEL GROUP PLC 1981 - 2002, third largest travel group in the world with revenues of £8 billion, 19 million customers, 25 tour operator brands, 4,500 travel agencies, a fleet of 90 aircraft and 40,000 staff worldwide. Sales markets in U.K., Germany, France, Benelux, Austria, Hungary, Poland, Canada, Egypt and India.

Following takeover by Euro Leisure Group plc, was appointed to develop international strategy and build multi-channel distribution businesses across Europe and North America.

MAIN ACHIEVEMENTS

MAIN ACHIEVEMENTS

- Conceived and developed new distribution channels in U.K., Europe and North America.
- Determined pan-European retail channel strategy and gained local country managers' commitment.
- Conducted strategic review of pan-European markets and gained sign off of multi-channel strategy.
- Identified £10m cost savings and restructuring opportunities across pan-European businesses.
- Developed and launched Canadian bilingual e-commerce travel site and call-centres.
- Led senior cross-functional teams, overseeing all aspects of products, retail and communications across company.
- Managed the rapid expansion of travelgroup.com, which is today rated within top 3 best and most frequently visited U.K. travel sites.

DIRECTOR, U.K. DEVELOPMENT - 1998-2000

Promoted to direct significant profit improvement initiatives and strategic change management programmes.

- Exceeded £14m profit improvement goal and all customer satisfaction targets.
- Led senior cross-functional teams with responsibility for all U.K. Sales, Productivity, Profit, Customer Service and CRM improvement programmes.
- Drove the U.K. multi-channel distribution strategy for Flights and component travel, leading to creation of travelgroup.com.
- Led joint venture negotiations with Independent Travel Agents that represents over 900 agencies throughout the U.K. This long-term relationship generated significant additional sales of £10m and support for the business.
- Directed the design, development, trial and roll out of highly successful Travel Group Hypermarket stores (10,000 sq.ft. out of town travel hypermarkets), generating new sales of £35m.

HEAD OF U.K. SALES DEVELOPMENT - 1996-1998

Appointed to rapidly establish Travel Group plc as market leader for Flights and independent travel.

- Achieved sales in excess of £175m through motivating 30 Regional Managers, 800 Branch Managers and 4,000 staff.
- Developed, piloted and rolled out first radically different and highly successful 'New Retail Concept' shop format.
- Led strategic review of Foreign Exchange distribution (post-E.M.U. impact on future revenues and U.K. Sales Network) and all subsequent change management programmes. Also identified several new travel-related products and services to replace potential Foreign Exchange revenue losses.

REGIONAL SALES & OPERATIONS MANAGER, SURREY & SUSSEX - 1995-1996

Responsible for multi-site leadership and motivation of 23 Sales Managers and 225 staff, generating £97m sales.

- Consistently exceeded all Sales, Profit and Customer Satisfaction targets and in 1996 achieved 'Top U.K. Region' status with greatest profit increase and highest customer satisfaction improvement.

GLOBAL SALES & RELATIONSHIP MANAGER - WORLDWIDE AIRLINE PLC - 1993-1995

- Maximised Worldwide Airline corporate sales and developed key relationships and partnerships worldwide. Key markets: North America, Australasia, Far East, South Africa and Europe.
- Exceeded extremely stretching £106m sales target and key objectives, which delivered an additional £1m bottom line profit.

Regional Operations Management - Central & West London - 1988-1993

worldwide. Key markets: North America, Australasia, Far East, South Africa and Europe.
- Exceeded extremely stretching £106m sales target and key objectives, which delivered an
  additional £1m bottom line profit.

Regional Operations Management - Central & West London - 1988-1993

Retail Store Management - London & South East - 1985-1988

Various sales and operational leadership roles within Foreign Exchange, Tour Operations & Business Travel - 1981-1985

HOMELAND STORES plc. - Department Manager - 1978-1981

BIGFOUR BANK plc. - Foreign Exchange, Securities & Lending - 1975-1978

PROFESSIONAL DEVELOPMENT

• INSEAD - Executive Leadership Programme	2000
• ABTA Board Member	1998
• C.I.M. Advanced Marketing Course	1997
• Global Leaders Development Programme - Italy	1994
• Worldwide Airline - Putting People First programme	1993
• H.N.C. Business Studies - Finance and Marketing bias	1980

PERSONAL DETAILS

Date of Birth: 02 August 1965
Status: Married with one daughter
Full and clean driving licence

INTERESTS

Current Affairs, Travel, Sailing, Skiing, Tennis

EXAMPLE OF A FUNCTIONAL CV

Ian Pringle BA (Hons.)
77 Tintern Close, Orton Wistow, Peterborough, PE2 0XY
Tel: +44 (0)1733 888888 Fax: +44 (0)1733 888889 e-mail: ip@netcomuk.co.uk

OBJECTIVE

A senior management position with a focus on business development and international commercial activities.

PROFILE

A goal-orientated multi-site Development Director with a proven track-record of driving major international change and profit improvement initiatives in the travel and leisure industries.

SKILLS SUMMARY

- Leading and developing multi-site and e-commerce retail distribution businesses
- Conceiving and directing major strategic, operational change-management programmes at board level
- Analysing customer trends and financial data to improve margins, reduce costs and maximise profits
- Utilising exceptional problem-solving and decision-making abilities
- Communicating strategy and influencing and inspiring teams at all levels
- Building and leading strong cross-functional, multi-cultural teams
- Relationship management and business to business (B2B) sales development

MAJOR ACHIEVEMENTS TO DATE:

DEVELOPING OPPORTUNITIES

- Directed significant profit improvement initiatives and strategic change management programmes

MAJOR ACHIEVEMENTS TO DATE:

DEVELOPING OPPORTUNITIES

- Directed significant profit improvement initiatives and strategic change management programmes across £5 billion multi-site retail sales operations - exceeded £20m bottom-line profit improvement goal and all customer satisfaction targets
- Conducted strategic review of pan-European markets and gained sign off of multi-channel strategy
- Developed and launched a Canadian bilingual e-commerce travel site and call centres

STRATEGIC LEADERSHIP

- Led a strategic review of Foreign Exchange distribution and all subsequent change management programmes
- Identified several new travel-related products and services to replace potential Foreign Exchange revenue losses
- Drove the U.K. multi-channel distribution strategy for flights and component travel, leading to creation of travelco.com - consistently rated in the top 5 best and most frequently visited U.K. travel websites

COMMERCIAL NEGOTIATIONS

- Determined pan-European retail distribution strategy and identified joint venture partners
- Led joint venture negotiations with Independent Travel Agents that represents over 900 agencies throughout the U.K.; this long-term relationship generated significant additional sales and support for Travelco plc
- Led other significant and highly confidential JV and merger and acquisition discussions

SELLING & RELATIONSHIP MANAGEMENT

- Maximised Worldwide Airline corporate sales and developed key relationships and partnerships worldwide. Key markets: North America, Australasia, Far East, South Africa and Europe. Exceeded extremely stretching £150m sales target and key objectives which delivered an additional £2m bottom line profit
- Rapidly established Travelco plc as market leader for flights and independent travel through motivating 30 Regional Managers, 800 Branch Managers and 4,000 staff to achieve sales in excess of £190m target
- Exceeded B2B sales targets for all products sold: foreign exchange, global money transfers, tour operator holidays, business travel
- Bigger4 Bank: commercial loans, foreign exchange, drafts and telegraphic transfers
- Travelco: foreign exchange services and global money transfer products
- Travelco Holidays: selling direct to independent agents - London and East Anglia
- Big Motor Company: business travel sales (largest account in U.K. for Travelco)

FINANCIAL AWARENESS

- P&L responsibility for multi-site leadership and motivation of 23 Sales Managers and 225 staff, generating £102m sales. Consistently exceeded all sales, profit and customer satisfaction targets and in 1996 achieved 'Top U.K. Region' status with greatest profit increase and highest customer satisfaction improvement
- Led senior cross-functional teams with responsibility for improving all U.K. sales training, manager and staff pay & benefits schemes, sales productivity, profit, customer service and CRM
- Responsible for the rapid expansion of travelco.com distribution channels (web, Wap, Idtv) and led multi-functional mass market development teams

EMPLOYMENT HISTORY

The Travelco Group, eighth largest travel group in the world with revenues of £2.3 billion, 10 million customers, 20 tour operator brands, 2,000 travel agencies, a fleet of 14 aircraft and 10,000 staff worldwide.

EMPLOYMENT HISTORY

The Travelco Group, eighth largest travel group in the world with revenues of £2.3 billion, 10 million customers, 30 tour operator brands, 2,000 travel agencies, a fleet of 14 aircraft and 10,000 staff worldwide. Sales markets: U.K., Germany, France, Benelux, Austria, Hungary, Poland, Canada, Egypt and India

Head of International Development	2000-2001
U.K. Development Director	1998-2000
Head of U.K. Sales Development	1996-1998
Regional Sales & Operations Manager - Surrey & Sussex	1995-1996
Global Sales & Relationship Manager - Worldwide Airline	1993-1995
Regional Operations Manager - Central & West London	1988-1993
Retail Store Management - London & South East	1985-1988
Various sales and operational leadership roles within Foreign Exchange Tour Operations & Business Travel	1981-1985
Department Manager - Home Stores plc	1978-1981
Foreign exchange, securities & lending - Bigger4 Bank plc	1975-1978

PROFESSIONAL DEVELOPMENT

INSEAD - Executive Leadership Programme	2000
A.B.T.A. Board Member	1998
C.I.M. Advanced Marketing Course	1997
Global Leaders Programme: Strategic Planning and Leadership	1994
Worldwide Airline - Putting People First programme	1993
H.N.C. Business Studies - Finance and Marketing bias	1980

PERSONAL DETAILS

Date of Birth: 02 August 1965
Status: Married with one daughter
Interests: current affairs, travel, sailing, skiing, tennis, school governor

STEP 3 - PREPARE AN EFFECTIVE CAREER HISTORY

USING THE INTERNET

In the last five years the internet has become a very important medium for career changers. To enhance your chances of success your career history must be compatible with e-mail and the internet:

1. Maximise your CV's ability to be scanned easily. Large organisations and recruiting agencies use powerful scanning systems to store and then *read* for key words on your career history.

2. Use specific nouns and action verbs to describe yourself, your job, your experience and your achievements.

3. Remember, database search engines will look for specific words or for specific job titles and professional/educational qualifications, eg: Chartered Engineer, Human Resources Manager, Copywriter, M.B.A., Direct Marketer, French (for language fluency), etc.

4. Use terms/acronyms specific to your industry or sector, eg: Visual Basic, Java and C++, as an alternative to a general term such as 'programming languages'; and JIT and TQM instead of 'manufacturing methods'.

 Tip! Try this useful website: http://www.eresumes.com/index.html

(74)

USING THE INTERNET

5. Avoid company specific jargon/abbreviations that the database software may not recognise or may mix up, eg: BA, BAT, ATOL.

6. Use action verbs to describe your achievements, eg: developed, implemented, designed.

7. Quantify your successes in numbers, eg: *During a six-month period, increased product X sales revenue from £20,000 to £35,000 – the biggest sales increase for any regional manager in the history of the North West region.*

8. Most search engines will look for skill sets or competencies. These words provide the reader with some concrete evidence of competence. If you want your CV to be read then you must use achievement- or competence-based words to describe yourself. Here are a few examples of key words for interpersonal traits that may describe the sort of person you are: able to delegate; assertive; skilled; achieves deadlines; entrepreneur; flexible; customer-focused; team-builder; creative problem-solver.

9. Try to use more than one page. The search engine will use all of the information it obtains from your CV to establish if your skill set matches any of the available vacancies. A two-page resumé will usually allow you to provide more information.

USING THE INTERNET

TECHNICAL POINTERS

- E-mail transmits text in a format called the American Standard Code for Information Interchange (ASCII)
- Condense your career history into that format
- Remove normal word processing formats, eg: bold, shading, fancy bullets, symbols, borders and italics
- Use only what you can see on a standard keyboard to help with the successful transmission or scanning of your CV
- Generally, e-mail readers are set at a width of 60-65 characters, so make sure the lines of text in your CV are reduced to that length
- Create the right length with an *enter* or carriage return to avoid the scanner/reader wrapping the lines into a meaningless clutter
- Use a *common* font (ie: Times, Arial or Courier)
- Keep your font size to about 12, 13 or 14 point
- If responding to a specific advert or job posting on a website, type the job title and/or reference number in the *subject area* of your e-mail message
- Finally, before e-mailing your CV to a company or recruitment agency, e-mail a copy to yourself to see what the finished product looks like

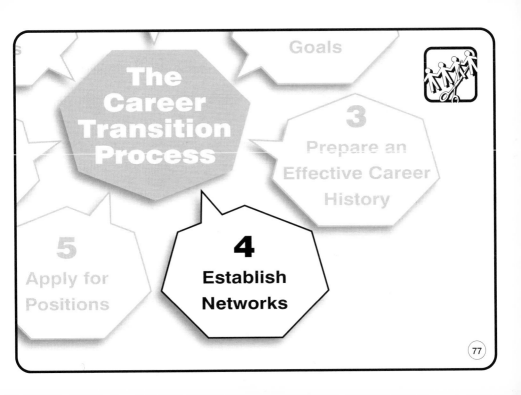

REACHING THE RIGHT PEOPLE

In the 1960s the American psychologist Dr Stanley Milgram posed this question: 'Can anyone in the world reach anyone else through a chain of only six friends?'

Networking is based on the principle of *six degrees of separation*, ie: the process of linking the people you know to the people the others know.

- Your next important step is to establish all the right networks to increase your chances of making your career change successful

- You must convince yourself that your next job will probably come either from your friends or from their friends

> *Never refuse any advance of friendship, for if nine out of ten bring you nothing, one alone may repay you.*
>
> **Madame de Tencin**

Tip! Try this website: http://www.wetfeet.com/advice/networking.asp; it provides a wealth of information about networking.

MAKE A LIST

Start your networking journey by putting together a 'Who do you know?' list. Who do you think they know?

FAMILY
COLLEGE
FRIENDS
CUSTOMERS
YOU
NEIGHBOURS
SUPPLIERS
CLUBS/SOCIETIES
MANAGERS

Start-up tips

- Build a list of all the people you think can help you in your career transition

- Put their names, addresses, phone numbers and e-mail addresses into a record system on file cards, a folder or, best of all, into a database on your computer

- Include sufficient space on your recording sheet for your comments on what was discussed

- Start thinking about your script for phone calls, meetings and e-mails

- Try to keep a simple but effective recording system

YOUR STRATEGY

Make your entire network of contacts an integral part of your job search. Your best approach is to write a script about what you may want to ask your contacts. Cover:

● Where you are now or what you are contemplating

● What has happened to you – redundancy, resignation, etc

● Those areas in which you think they may be able to offer you advice

● Information, ideas and solutions you wish to bounce off them

You can choose to write a letter, send e-mails, telephone them or arrange to meet them face-to-face.

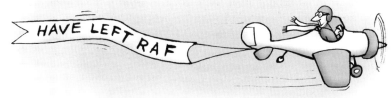

HAVE LEFT RAF

8 STEPS TO SUCCESS

The hardest part of networking is usually making that first telephone call or setting up the first meeting! When asked, most people going through change say they do not enjoy this phase.

Some useful tips:

1. Force yourself to use the telephone to contact people on your network list
2. Practise and learn to establish rapport – the process gets easier
3. State your purpose clearly/directly and listen more than you talk
4. Seek permission, ie: ask how much time they will allow you
5. Communicate your enthusiasm and keenness, and ask for their advice and ideas
6. Take lots of notes and, if possible, ask them for referrals to others
7. Aim to set up face-to-face meetings – your many friendly telephone calls will soon begin to produce results
8. When you are successful at obtaining meetings use steps 2 to 6 as your meeting template

STEP 4 - ESTABLISH NETWORKS

QUESTIONS TO ESTABLISH OPPORTUNITY

More tips to ensure your networking telephone calls and meetings are successful:

- Focus on anything change-related, because change means opportunity
- Ask for information about business trends, especially current developments in your functional area or field
- Find out about plans for new products or services
- Establish which new markets are emerging
- Most organisations do not advertise every vacancy so find out about the hidden jobs, about the departments that might be trying to hire people and about forthcoming retirements
- If you are really interested in the organisation ask for insider tips about corporate culture
- If possible, ask for information about any likely reorganisations, expansions, mergers or acquisitions
- Find out about any trade associations, journals or websites

QUESTIONS BEFORE AN INTERVIEW

If you have an interview coming up, and you have a contact with inside information of that prospective employer, here are some questions you may like to ask him/her:

- What is a typical day? How varied are the jobs that you do?
- What originally drew you to this job/career?
- What are the most rewarding tasks you have done since joining the company?
- What do you like most/least about your job?
- Do you feel that your work is recognised as an individual or as part of a team?
- How would you describe the work environment?
- Is there anything you would like to change about your job or the company?
- What selection process did you have to go through to get your job?
- Are there opportunities for further training/development?

 Tip! If you are interviewed, you can ask the same sort of questions at the end of your interview

NETWORKING TIPS

Some final words:

- Networking is an acquired skill that requires courage and practice
- We aren't born knowing how to network successfully but we can learn
- Try to smile, play a role, pool resources, reach out and ask as many questions as you can – this is the route to success
- After you have worked hard to get what you want, don't forget to say a big THANK YOU to all those who helped you
- If you are successful then remember to help someone else in the future if they ask for help

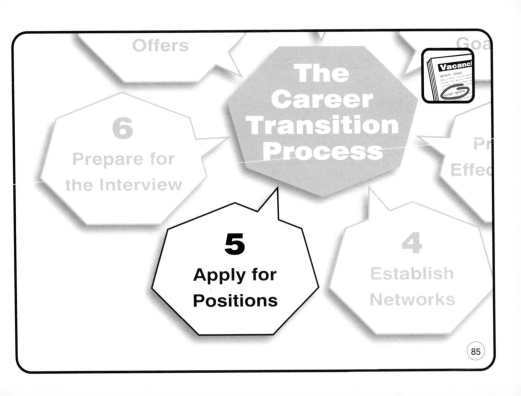

MARKETING YOURSELF

Having prepared your Career History and done some extensive networking research it is time to start your job search in earnest.

Think of yourself as a product – in other words, **market yourself!**

Self-marketing means making sure that anyone recruiting knows about your skills and achievements.

Experience shows that the rigorous, proven principles and processes of marketing are as relevant to you as they are to any product.

If you don't tell them how good you are, no one else will!

We can do anything we want if we stick to it long enough.

Helen Keller

STEP 5 - APPLY FOR POSITIONS

COVER LETTERS

Cover letters are the key to effective marketing.

By now you should have a plan of action for your job search, one that suits your personal situation and goals.

Having identified your objectives and designed your CV you now need one further piece of marketing literature and then you are ready to launch your product *(PRODUCT YOU)* onto the market.

A covering letter is the most effective method to prompt a recruiter to read your CV.

A well-worded letter demonstrates that you understand all the features and requirements of the job you are applying for.

The cover letter allows you to explain why you want to work in that area, and shows how your skills, experience and achievements match the vacancy.

LETTER TEMPLATES

Some templates for the ideal cover letters:

1
Start with your interest in the job

Market yourself - what you have to offer in terms of skills and achievements

Give some more detail about your job

Tell them what you hope will happen next

End on an appreciative note

2
Start by telling them what you know about the company and why you wish to apply for a job there

Say what you can do for them

Tell them what you have done and how well you have done it

Tell them what you are worth now and what you are expecting to be paid

End on a positive note

STEP 5 - APPLY FOR POSITIONS

LETTER TEMPLATES

3 Use the name of a network contact to set the scene in your first paragraph

Provide them with some background about yourself

Tell them what you have done and how well you have done it

Tell them what you hope will happen next

End on an appreciative note

4 Tell them why you admire them/their company

Tell them what you can do for them

Tell them why you are applying - redundancy, restructure, relocation, etc

Tell them what you are worth now and what you are expecting to be paid

Tell them what you hope will happen next and thank them

APPLICATION FOR A JOB IN RESPONSE TO A NEWSPAPER ADVERT

Example 1
Some guidelines
on what to write

Peter Browning, 25 Windsor Lane, Bramley, Leeds LS17 2UU
Tel: 0113 222 4466, Mobile: 07990 333112, E-mail: pb3203@hotwire.com

Mr. Iain Blackman - Managing Director
Plexus Plastics
Hyde Technology Park
Manchester
MA16 2FF

Dear Mr Blackman

I read your advertisement for a Senior Chemist in the Manchester Evening News
with a great deal of interest. I am writing to apply for this challenging role because
I believe that I have all of the skills you require for this role. I am enclosing a
complete Career History outlining my professional qualifications and achievements
for your review and consideration.

As you read my CV, I am sure you will see that my qualifications should allow me to
add hugely to the overall efficiency and productivity of Plexus' R & D efforts through
the application of various process methods. By training your R & D chemists in
empirically-based experimental design, plant layout modelling can be implemented
with much greater precision and consistency. In my previous role as Senior Chemist
with Cambridge Innovation Plastics, I developed and implemented a Styrofoam
extrusion process that recycled 75% of the waste products and resulted in a 20%
increase in productivity and savings of £120,000 in 2000.

> Start with your
> interest in the job

> Market yourself, ie:
> what you have to offer
> in terms of skills and
> achievements

the application of various process methods. By training your ... ...

empirically-based experimental design, plant layout modelling can be implemented

with much greater precision and consistency. In my previous role as Senior Chemist

with Cambridge Innovation Plastics, I developed and implemented a Styrofoam extrusion process that recycled 75% of the waste products and resulted in a 20% increase in productivity and savings of £120,000 in 2000.

My academic experience includes a Ph.D. in Applied Chemistry and over 20 years' research and development experience working in three competitor companies. I am thoroughly conversant with the design of chemical plant equipment and layout. In my previous role I managed a team of 10 chemists and 8 laboratory and administrative staff.

I would really welcome the opportunity to discuss further how my experience can make an immediate difference to the success of Plexus Plastics. I will call within the next couple of days to determine your interest and, if appropriate, to arrange for a personal meeting at your convenience.

Yours sincerely

Give some more detail about your Background summary

Tell them what you hope will happen next

APPLICATION FOR A PLACE ON A GRADUATE DEVELOPMENT SCHEME

Example 2
Some guidelines
on what to write

Sally Ford, 62 Wineglass Cottage, Church Lane, Boxley, Kent ME14 3NN
Tel: 01622 854466, Mobile: 07888 333112, E-mail: s.ford3107@hotwire.com

Mrs. J Wild – HR Manager
Mid Kent Utility
Rocland Road
Maidstone
Kent ME2 5AH

Dear Mrs Wild

> Start by telling them what you know about the company and why you would like to apply for a job there. Remember to say nice things about the company!

I recently saw a copy of your very informative graduate recruitment brochure in the Careers Office at the University of Luton. It states that you recruit Accounting Trainees every year. I am very keen to gain a place on a graduate scheme with such an excellent reputation as yours. One of my neighbours works in the Marketing Department and has told me what a great company it is to work for. I am therefore very interested in gaining an interview with you during your forthcoming 'milk round' recruiting trip to the University of Luton.

For your information:
I will graduate with a First or 2:1 BSc degree in Accounting this June

Tell them what you have done and how well you have done it

For your information:

- I will graduate with a First or 2:1 BSc degree in Accounting this June
- I can state confidently that I have been a dedicated student and have been recognised by the University for my academic achievements through the receipt of various awards, the details of which are shown on my enclosed curriculum vitae.
- As my CV shows, I have been continually employed, either full- or part-time, since the age of thirteen in jobs dealing with figures and handling cash.
- Despite my heavy workload, I have also managed to squeeze in a healthy choice of external sporting and charity activities because of my ability to effectively plan and manage my time.
- My sound academic accomplishments, strong work ethic, drive, organisation skills, and passion for the accounting discipline will hopefully convince you that I have the basic ingredients to make a valuable contribution to the Company's graduate scheme.

End on an appreciative note

I hope you are impressed with what you see on my CV and I look forward to meeting you at the recruiting interviews. Thank you.

Yours sincerely

UNSOLICITED APPLICATION USING A NETWORKING CONTACT'S NAME

Example 3
Some guidelines
on what to write

Debbie Ashford, 36 Hillcrest Avenue, Wicken, Nr Milton Keynes MK12 3YT
Tel: 01908 224567, Mobile: 07333 234567 E-mail: dashford@cix.co.uk

Miss Caroline Denning
Keep Safe Data Limited
Chapel Street
Bletchley MK21 IBS

Dear Miss Denning

During a recent conversation with your Administration Director, Matt Stevenson, I was advised that you are considering implementing a Business Process Re-engineering programme at Keep Safe Data, and may be looking for a keen Project Manager to lead this major undertaking. Should you be seeking such a manager, you may well want to consider me for this assignment.

I have just completed a full-time MBA with Warwick University, but over the last 12 years I have worked in London for a major Consulting company, especially in the field of process improvement. I have wide experience of implementing innovative strategies for achieving broader process flexibility, streamlining operations and workflow.

> Use the name of a network contact to set the scene in your first paragraph

Project Manager to lead this major undertaking. Should you be seeking such a manager, you may well want to consider me for this assignment.

Provide some background about yourself

I have just completed a full-time MBA with Warwick University, but over the last 15 years I have worked in London for a major Consulting company, especially in the field of process improvement. I have wide experience of implementing innovative strategies for achieving broader process flexibility, streamlining operations and reducing costs in information capture, document management and workflow.

Tell them what you have done and how well you have done it

I have provided the overall leadership to a highly successful business-wide BPR initiative at Winston Insurance which resulted in a substantial (£10 million) improvement to business performance this year alone. I would welcome the challenge of undertaking a similar effort at Keep Safe.

Tell them what you hope will happen next

I will call you next week to find out if you are interested in discussing this matter and, if appropriate, to arrange a meeting with you.

End on an appreciative note

I have heard some excellent things from Matt about the exciting future at Keep Safe, and I look forward to the possibility of meeting you personally.

Yours sincerely

UNSOLICITED APPLICATION

Example 4
Some guidelines
on what to write

Paul Manning, Dandy Bush Farm, Melton Deeping, Lincs PE18 2QQ
Tel: 01778 234567, Mobile: 07321 223344, E-mail: manningp@biznet.com

Mr. William Wilson
Chief Executive
Webworld Science
Technology Park Circle
Cambridge CB12 3FF

Dear Mr. Wilson

> Flattery can be useful
> as a good start point

I know that you, as a well-recognised entrepreneur of a leading UK technology company, are aware of the importance of having a go-ahead Finance Director to handle the financial challenges of a successful and growing enterprise. If you are in need of such an individual, you may want to consider my experience.

> Tell them what you can
> do for them

I am a qualified CIMA management accountant with over fifteen years' experience in electronics manufacturing. I am proud to have achieved some significant successes in such important areas as the low-cost capitalisation of major expansions and acquisitions, significant cash flow improvement, debt reduction and significant MI reporting improvements. In my current position I recently led a corporate-wide cost reduction project that contributed nearly 30% (£3m) profit improvement in the last year alone.

reduction and significant MI reporting improvements. In my current position I recently led a corporate-wide cost reduction project that contributed nearly 30% (£3M) profit improvement in the last year alone.

Despite this success, I realise that I must find another job in the near future. I work for a relatively small family-run business and I recognise that my career prospects are fairly limited.

> Tell them why you are applying – redundancy, restructure, relocation, etc

For your information my current salary is £55,000 plus bonuses and car, and I am looking for a similar role that pays in the region of £60-65K.

> Tell them what you are worth now and what you are expecting to be paid

If you are looking for a results-driven senior finance manager with a significant track record of achievement, then I would appreciate the opportunity to prove to you that I have all the skills and experience you are seeking. I look forward to hearing from you in the near future. Thank you.

> Tell them what you hope will happen next and thank them

Yours sincerely

STEP 5 - APPLY FOR POSITIONS

PUTTING IT ALL INTO PRACTICE

You now have:
- A great Career History (hard copy and/or online version)
- Some well-worded cover letters (hard copy and/or online versions)

You are now ready to apply for *real* jobs in the following ways:

1. Responding to advertisements in newspapers and professional magazines
2. Approaching recruitment/search and selection agencies by letter, e-mail or telephone
3. Applying online directly to companies or recruitment sites
4. Using networking contacts to gain introductions to companies or recruiters
5. Directly contacting companies/organisations that you choose through your research
6. Via Job Centres

Good luck with your applications!

Tip! When posting your cover letter and CV do not fold them. Use a full size (C4) envelope. Use quality paper if you can, eg: white or high white laid Conqueror 100gsm or the equivalent.

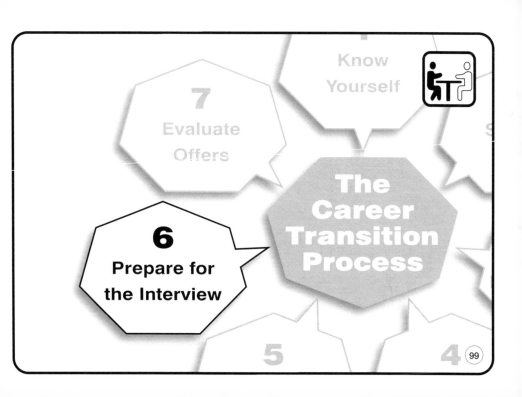

STEP 6 - PREPARE FOR THE INTERVIEW

CONVERSATION WITH A PURPOSE

Well done – you have been invited to an interview!

For most people this invitation is the point at which *panic* sets in. But, remember:

- An interview is just a *conversation with a purpose* – a very important conversation but simply a conversation after all
- It is normally inevitable for most jobs
- If you follow certain rules you can enhance your chances of success
- The effective interviewer should want you to help him/her solve a problem, ie: fill the vacancy
- It is a two-way process for both parties to find out about each other
- It can sometimes change your life forever
- Quite often the interviewer is just as nervous as you are

> *The interviewer should just tell me the words he wants me to say and I'll repeat them after him.*

Andy Warhol

WHAT YOU MUST DO BEFORE THE INTERVIEW

One absolute must is **P.R.E.P**

P LAN

R ESEARCH

E XPECT

P RACTISE

STEP 6 - PREPARE FOR THE INTERVIEW

P.R.E.P - PLAN

Your PLAN should consist of:

- Tasks you must do before the interview, eg: confirm that you will attend the interview
- A list of contacts you should talk to before the interview, eg: someone who works in the company and may know the interviewer and his/her style of interviewing
- Interview tactics
- Questions to ask the interviewer
- Strategy concerning what salary you will ask for
- How you will get to the interview in good time
- What you will wear on the day
- Your thank you letter!

STEP 6 - PREPARE FOR THE INTERVIEW

P.R.E.P - RESEARCH

You should RESEARCH absolutely **everything** you need to know about the company and the job:

- Ask for a copy of the job description/person specification if you have not already done so

- Ask for any company brochures, journals and the company annual accounts if they exist

- Look up the company/organisation on the internet if they have a website

- Print off any interesting information about philosophy, products, services, prices, successes, recent news, etc

- Talk to your network contacts – they may have very useful inside information about the company/organisation

P.R.E.P - RESEARCH

- Ask your network contacts for advice about interview techniques
- Research the job description – be sure you understand exactly what the job requirements are
- If you know someone who works in the company or, better still, the relevant department, ask for information about the company
- If you do not have access to a computer then visit your local library – there is usually a reference section with Business and Organisation Directories
- There is usually a good Reference Library in every major city and most large towns; don't be afraid to ask a librarian for help, they are usually very helpful

Whatever you do, do something! Remember, *If you fail to plan, then you plan to fail!*

 Tip! A very good site for interview preparation is www.bbc.co.uk/radio1/essentials/work/interviews. But there are many more. Just type in 'PREPARE FOR A JOB INTERVIEW' on a well-known search engine.

P.R.E.P - EXPECT

You know with certainty that you will be interviewed so you should try to work out what sort of questions to EXPECT in the interview.

Some little known facts you should know about interviews:

- Many interviews are a lottery; sometimes it depends on how the interviewer feels that day
- You have to work hard at making sure that the *chemistry* between you and the interviewer is right
- Not all interviewers have an acceptable level of skills to get the best from you
- Many interviewers make their *yes/no* decisions within five minutes of meeting you
- There are several different types of interviews – in your planning and research, try to find out which type of interview it is

Tip! www.quintcareers.com is a must visit website! It has many terrific tips to help you with your preparation.

P.R.E.P - EXPECT

WHAT YOU CAN EXPECT IN ALMOST EVERY INTERVIEW

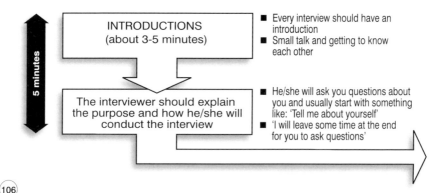

5 minutes

INTRODUCTIONS
(about 3-5 minutes)

- Every interview should have an introduction
- Small talk and getting to know each other

The interviewer should explain the purpose and how he/she will conduct the interview

- He/she will ask you questions about you and usually start with something like: 'Tell me about yourself'
- 'I will leave some time at the end for you to ask questions'

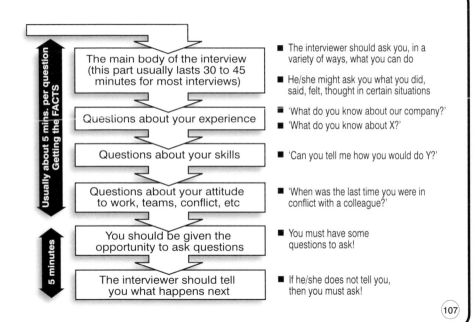

STEP 6 - PREPARE FOR THE INTERVIEW

P.R.E.P - EXPECT

EXPECT one of the following:

- Traditional interview
- Panel interview
- Behavioural (competence) interview

- Extended interview process,
  eg: presentation, psychometric tests,
  meet the team, a site visit, etc

In a traditional interview expect anything. However, the usual areas covered are:

- Introductory or general questions
- Your management experience
- Your motivation
- How you handle conflict
- How you deal with customers/
  colleagues

- An opportunity for you to ask questions
- Education/Work
- Your skills and competences
- Why you are leaving your company
- What should happen next

Two 'killer' questions to ask in the interview to help you to sell yourself:
1. After 5-10 minutes ask: 'What sort of skills are you looking for in the ideal candidate?'
2. At the closing stages ask: 'Am I the sort of person you are looking for?'

STEP 6 - PREPARE FOR THE INTERVIEW

P.R.E.P - EXPECT

BEHAVIOUR OR COMPETENCY BASED INTERVIEW

Behaviour or competency based interview questions usually start with:

- 'Tell me about a time when...'
- 'Describe a situation where...'
- 'Give me a specific example of...'

The interviewer might *signpost* the behaviour/competency content of the question by saying something like: 'This job requires you to deal on occasion with very angry or difficult customers. Tell me about a time when you had to deal with a very angry customer'. You must describe the situation, after which...

The interviewer follows up with probes like:

'What happened then? What did you say? What happened after that? How was it resolved? How did you feel? What did you learn from that experience? Who else knew about what happened? Were you commended/criticised for your actions?'

Overall, a very different sort of interview but, luckily, one that you can plan for!

STEP 6 - PREPARE FOR THE INTERVIEW

P.R.E.P - EXPECT

BEHAVIOUR OR COMPETENCY BASED INTERVIEW

Example questions:
- Tell me about a time when you were able to use your influencing skills to convince a colleague to accept your point of view
- Describe a time when you were faced with a stressful situation that showed your ability to deal with pressure
- Tell me of a time when you used your analytical skills to solve a complex problem
- Give me an example of a time when you had to work to a very tight deadline
- Tell me about a time when you had to make a presentation to a group of people who probably did not want to hear what you had to say
- Give me a specific example of a time when you had to sell to others a policy with which you did not agree
- Tell me about a time when you had to go above and beyond the call of duty in order to satisfy a really difficult customer

You can then usually expect follow-up with probing questions like:
'What did you do? What did you say? What happened then? What did that achieve? How did you feel? What did you learn? What would you do differently if it happened again?'

P.R.E.P - PRACTISE

The final stage of **P.R.E.P** is PRACTISE.

If you want to succeed then you must:

1. PRACTISE, PRACTISE , PRACTISE
    your newly acquired interview
    techniques as often as you can
    prior to the interview

2. Depending on the type of interview
    you are expecting, and the sort
    of role you are being interviewed
    for, then you must PRACTISE
    answering a range of interview
    questions

P.R.E.P - PRACTISE

Some tips to help you:
- Try writing out some questions and model answers
- Even better, use a computer to record everything electronically (the same sort of questions recur time and time again)
- Practise mock interviews with friend, partner, colleague or mentor
- If you can't find a partner use a tape recorder or, better still, a video camera to record your mock interviews; time yourself
- Do not take too long to answer a question, no more than two or three minutes each
- For behaviour/competency interviews try to recall as many examples of achievements, tasks, projects and occasions where you have excelled at something

 Tip! There are some excellent websites to help you with your interview practice, eg:
http://www.meetit.com/intvtque.html,
http://www.careerperfect.com/CareerPerfect/interviewFAQs.htm and
http://www.r360.net/InterviewTips.html
There are also many books on how to prepare for interviews. Try a quick search on
www.amazon.co.uk

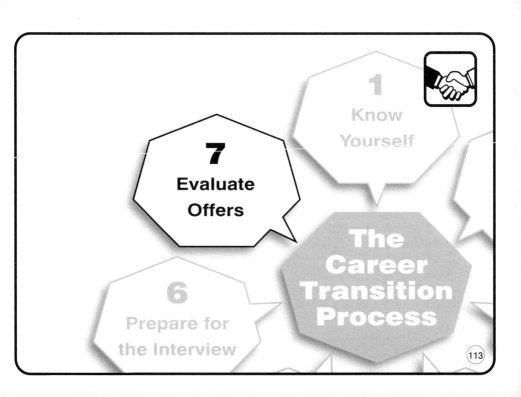

7
Evaluate
Offers

1
Know
Yourself

6
Prepare for
the Interview

The Career Transition Process

STEP 7 - EVALUATE OFFERS

STOP & THINK

Congratulations! You have just received a job offer by telephone or letter! What happens now? The first piece of advice is – stop and think! Accepting a job offer is a major decision which can affect your life and others close to you in a number of important ways. Some tips:

- Don't say *yes* to a job offer instantly; take your time and go over all your choices.
- Think about your choices wisely and assess the job offer and how it matches your career goals.
- If you receive an offer, but you are still waiting to hear from other employers, then be open and honest with the person who has offered you the job.
- Explain your position and ask for more time (a week or even more) to decide.
- Don't wait until the last minute to ask for extra time; this might appear to be procrastination and will suggest lack of planning skills on your part.
- Be positive about the offer, be polite, and be sensitive about what you say, because if you finally accept you could end up working for that person!
- Call the other employers to tell them that you have an offer in writing. Ask them to confirm when they intend to make a decision.
- Stop the interviewing process once you have made up your mind. It is unethical and unprofessional to accept another offer if you have said *yes* to another party.

SALARY NEGOTIATIONS: A USEFUL MODEL

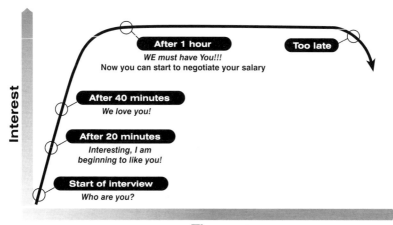

SALARY NEGOTIATIONS

Some DO'S and DON'TS:

Do
Think about what salary you are prepared to accept long before it is raised
Keep up with latest salary trends in your sector and the job market in general
Take **every component of your salary expectations** into consideration when negotiating, eg: pensions, bonuses, health insurance, company cars, travelling costs, etc
Negotiate on the basis of the responsibilities of the job and your future performance in the job
Have a realistic salary range in mind, eg: 'I was thinking somewhere in the range of £XX,000 to £YY,000'
Behave in a professional and courteous manner when you are negotiating

Do Not
Raise salary expectations early on in the interview unless you know you are at the **'We must have you'** phase
Overestimate your importance to the company - be realistic about your expectations
Negotiate if you know you are not really interested in the company or the job
Specify a single salary figure when asked 'What are your salary requirements?'
Accept a job until you receive the offer in writing
Fall out with the person making the offer. You may want to work there in the future!

A SAMPLE LETTER OF ACCEPTANCE

Paul Stead - Human Resources Manager
SB Insurance Ltd
SB House, Venture Way

May 4, 200-

Dear Mr Stead

Thank you for your written offer of employment as a Customer Service Team Manager at SB Insurance Ltd. I am really delighted to accept your salary offer of £27,000 per annum plus performance bonuses. I look forward to beginning work on 10 June 200- at SB House.

I have signed all the documents you required but please let me know if I need to provide you with any further information.

Again, thank you for offering me this exciting opportunity. I look forward to working at SB Insurance.

Yours sincerely

A SAMPLE LETTER DECLINING AN OFFER

Steven Fletcher - Senior Chemist
Alliance Plastics
Larchwood House
Cambridge CB2 2SD

May 4, 200-

Dear Mr Fletcher

Thank you for your offer for the position of Research Chemist in the R & D Department. After very careful consideration I have decided to accept a similar position with another plastics company based a short distance from my home.

I believe this opportunity is a better match with my research and development interests, and would involve no relocation upheaval.

Thank you again for the time you spent showing me around the site last month. I really appreciate the interest you showed in me, and I enjoyed learning about the interesting challenges you face at Alliance.

Yours sincerely

A GREAT QUOTE FROM TOM PETERS

> *You don't 'belong to' any company for life, and your chief affiliation isn't to any particular 'function'. You're not defined by your job title, and you're not confined by your job description.*
>
> *Your 'career' is yours alone to define, yours alone to change, and yours alone to assess - as often and truthfully as you wish.*
>
> *Begin now. Begin here.*

119

FURTHER READING

Search on www.amazon.co.uk for the following books or ask for them at a bookshop:

Barrie Hopson and Mike Scally, *Build Your Own Rainbow*

Richard N Bolles, *What Color Is Your Parachute? A Practical Manual for Job-Hunters and Career-Changers*

Jason R. Rich, *Job Hunting For The Utterly Confused*

Jon Warner, *The Networking Pocketbook*

Max A. Eggert, *The Perfect Interview*

Deb Gottesman, Buzz Mauro, *The Interview Rehearsal Book - 7 Steps to Job-Winning Interviews Using Acting Skills You Never Knew You Had*

Martin John Yate, *Great Answers to Tough Interview Questions*

Dana Morgan, *7 Minute Cover Letters*

Martin Yate & Terra Dourlain, *Online Job Hunting*

Margaret Riley Dikel & Frances Roehm, *Guide To Internet Job Searching 2002 - 2003*

USEFUL JOB SITES

At the time of writing, the websites shown here were very popular sites for career change and job hunting. But there are hundreds more – just keep searching!

Click A Job	www.clickajob.com
Fish4.com	www.fish4.co.uk/jobs/index.jsp
Gis-a-job.com	www.gis-a-job.com
GoJobSite	www.gojobsite.co.uk
Jobpilot	www.jobpilot.co.uk
MonsterBoard	www.monster.co.uk
StepStone	www.stepstone.co.uk
Top Jobs	www.topjobs.co.uk
Totaljobs	www.totaljobs.com
Workthing.com	www.workthing.com
Alljobsuk.com	www.alljobsuk.com
Btopenworld	www.btopenworld.com/jobs
Careers Portal	www.careersportal.co.uk
GIS Employment Service	www.employmentservice.gov.uk
Employment Backbone	www.iesolutions.net/backbone.htm
Jobs.co.uk	www.jobs.co.uk
Britain's Job Agent	www.jobs-in-the-uk.com/
UK Jobs Guide	www.ukjobsguide.co.uk

About the Author

Keith Corbin, BA (Hons), MCIM
Keith has been employed as a freelance Career Coach and
management trainer for the last seven years. He is now currently
in his third career, having spent 15 years as an engineer in the
Royal Navy and sixteen years in a variety of HR roles with the
Thomas Cook Group. He is particularly proud of project managing
the most comprehensive change management programme
undertaken by the Thomas Cook Group in its history (The People
Like Us - PLUS Programme).

Keith has gained over 24 years' experience of Human Resource and Organisation
Development consulting and since leaving Thomas Cook has applied those skills in a
variety of business sectors, eg: travel, food manufacturing, automotive, financial services,
retail fashion, electronic engineering, the civil service and local authorities.

He is particularly keen on the use of computers in business, and sees the internet as a
major force for change especially in relation to career transition. A CD ROM on all
aspects of career transition is available as an additional resource to this pocketbook.

Contact
Keith can be contacted by e-mail at: info@career-transition.co.uk
Also see: www.career-transition.co.uk

ORDER FORM

Your details

Name _____

Position _____

Company _____

Address _____

_____

Telephone _____

Fax _____

E-mail _____

VAT No. (EC companies) _____

Your Order Ref _____

Please send me:

	No. copies
The Career Transition Pocketbook	[ ]
The _____ Pocketbook	[ ]
The _____ Pocketbook	[ ]
The _____ Pocketbook	[ ]
The _____ Pocketbook	[ ]

Order by Post

MANAGEMENT POCKETBOOKS LTD

LAUREL HOUSE, STATION APPROACH, ALRESFORD,
HAMPSHIRE SO24 9JH UK

Order by Phone, Fax or Internet

Telephone: +44 (0)1962 735573
Facsimile: +44 (0)1962 733637
E-mail: sales@pocketbook.co.uk
Web: www.pocketbook.co.uk

Customers in USA should contact:
Stylus Publishing, LLC, 22883 Quicksilver Drive,
Sterling, VA 20166-2012
Telephone: 703 661 1581 or 800 232 0223
Facsimile: 703 661 1501 E-mail: styluspub@aol.com

THE MANAGEMENT POCKETBOOK SERIES

Pocketbooks

Appraisals
Assertiveness
Balance Sheet
Business Planning
Business Presenter's
Business Writing
Career Transition
Challengers
Coaching
Communicator's
Controlling Absenteeism
Creative Manager's
C.R.M.
Cross-cultural Business
Cultural Gaffes
Customer Service
Decision-making
Developing People
Discipline
E-commerce
E-customer Care

Emotional Intelligence
Empowerment
Facilitator's
Handling Complaints
Improving Efficiency
Improving Profitability
Induction
Influencing
International Trade
Interviewer's
Key Account Manager's
Learner's
Manager's
Managing Budgets
Managing Cashflow
Managing Change
Managing Upwards
Managing Your Appraisal
Marketing
Meetings
Mentoring

Motivation
Negotiator's
Networking
People Manager's
Performance Management
Personal Success
Project Management
Problem Behaviour
Quality
Sales Excellence
Salesperson's
Self-managed Development
Starting In Management
Stress
Teamworking
Telephone Skills
Telesales
Thinker's
Time Management
Trainer Standards
Trainer's

Pocketsquares

Great Presentation Scandal
Great Training Robbery
Hook Your Audience
Leadership: Sharing The Passion

Pocketfiles

Trainer's Blue Pocketfile of
Ready-to-use Exercises

Trainer's Green Pocketfile of
Ready-to-use Exercises

Trainer's Red Pocketfile of
Ready-to-use Exercises

Audio Cassettes

Tips for Presenters
Tips for Trainers